KISS
SPIRIT

Doug Norgren and Barb Lund

ISBN 979-8-88616-928-7 (paperback)
ISBN 979-8-88616-929-4 (digital)

Christian Faith Publishing
832 Park Avenue
Meadville, PA 16335
www.christianfaithpublishing.com

Printed in the United States of America

Choose a Life of Recovery
SOS [1, 2, 3]
It's As Simple As A, B, C, D

Gettin' awoke by the stench of skunk at five in the morning, I am motivated to start writing again in my book.

What a motivator! The aroma of skunk woke me up a few hours earlier than I planned. This stench got me to light a candle, turn on the coffee pot, then take a pee, and smoke a cigarette, all in the normal time it takes me to get my eyes open and my feet on the floor for the first time.

Let me explain. At the present moment, I am hanging my hat in an eight-by-eight room inside a four-car garage. In my room, I have a refrigerator and two microwaves. I have no stove, and the nearest running water source is two hundred feet away. My coffee water is ready to go in a nearby Igloo cooler with a spigot. There were stretches this winter when I had a five-gallon block of ice with a handle on it. I'll leave my number-two morning sit-down concerns to your imagination.

What I am grateful for in my living arrangement is why I live where I do. Gratitude is a magical attitude. My abovementioned living concerns take a back seat to what I am grateful for at my place of residence. I am grateful for the shelter of my two vehicles and two snowmobiles along with my belongings.

About eighteen months ago, I had one ride and walked three blocks to chase it down. Two blocks straight up the hill. I am grateful for no longer living in the ghetto as now I am in a small, small town. I am grateful for all the unconditional love around me.

Three cats named Spook, Kissy Kitty, and Ooofta Kitty. Clawhickys are welcome. Other critters roaming the property are two dogs, two sometimes three rabbits, a yard full of birds, a very compassionate landlord, and varying numbers of deer from one day to the next. I can choose to dwell on the downside of where I live or focus on the positives. I choose to concentrate on the positives and remain grateful for them.

My name is Doug Norgren and I wrote this book to trigger *sober-mind* thoughts in order to drown out all your *alcoholic-mind* thoughts with fun and effective acronyms found throughout. I want you to become consumed with HOPE as you read this book.

Gratitude is accompanied by HOPE always.

{H}ang

{O}nto

{P}ositive

{E}xpectations always. Keeping a grateful attitude and hanging onto positive expectations will get you anywhere. Of course, one must put forth continual action and effort for those expectations to become reality. FAITH WITHOUT WORKS will get you nowhere. In recovery, I choose to live with gratitude and hope in my heart. Consumed with the two of them, daily conscious choices were made. One day at a time. One moment at a time.

The Bible says, "Then touched he their eyes, saying, according to your faith be it onto you. And their eyes were opened" (Mathew 9:29–30).

We must remain in a state of hope—hope for a sober life. All we do is an inside job. A change of mindset—a mindset of hope instead of despair. If you track with me throughout this book, I truly believe you will gain an overwhelming hope for yourself in attaining a sober life filled with your very own wishes and dreams. If I can do this, you and anyone else can.

I was a functioning alcoholic for years. Dating back to my booty, bottle, bag, bartending college days, and decades thereafter. After a handful of DUIs (drinking under the influence), I finally found myself in a treatment center for alcoholism.

My first four DUIs were spaced out every five years give or take, and back then, the laws were less strict so I was never court-ordered to treatment or even AA. When I got my fifth DUI, I knew treatment was my destiny as laws had become more punishing since my fourth driving while drunk. With concerned help/intervention from my mom and a best friend, I surrendered myself voluntarily to inpatient treatment even before my court proceedings started. Now with jail time possible and probable, I had a tremendous motivator to change my mindset from denial to reality that I needed to do something about my drinking.

I had actually prayed for divine help before getting that fifth DUI. I had become sick and tired of being sick and tired. About being physically dependent on my sauce of choice, MY BLUE MISTRESS, Milwaukee's Best Ice, to the tune of between one and two cases a days, seven days a week for years.

My simple prayer to God was done on my hands and knees with only a mustard seed of hope and faith. At the time I thought there might be a God, but how forgiving he may be was also in question to me. I had very rarely gone to church in twenty years but for holidays, funerals, weddings, etc. All I knew for sure was that after being a functioning alcoholic for years and drinking turning into a full-time job with lots of overtime every week for about five years, I became sick and tired of being sick and tired. I was ready and wanted to be a retired functioning alcoholic.

That was the key, *my want to*. I wanted out, and GOD ALMIGHTY knew it! Has anyone ever heard that God knows our every thought? He answered my prayer because I was sincere in my asking. He knew that I had a change of heart about my drinking. DUI number 5 was the answer to my prayer. My cry for help.

There were no cars on the road for miles. Being a smoker, a person has a puff while driving, right? I had dotted my *I*s and crossed my *T*s before I lit up. I looked in the rear view mirror, and there was not a single car behind me. Oncoming traffic was also a notta. While lighting up I went over the passenger side fog line on the road. No biggie. Maybe a foot. I got my cig lit, and on I motored for about five miles into town without seeing a car behind me or approaching. I drove that stretch of the road enjoying my cigarette and not straying from my lane of driving. About two blocks from my home, flashing squad car lights are now right behind me. That police car was dropped down from the skies above. It came out of nowhere. I reached for my life-savor breath mints on the passenger seat of my car and proceed to pull over. Our *alcoholic minds* are great, aren't they? That breath mint did not do shit for the odor of alcohol sweating through the pores of my skin. It was summertime, and perspiring profusely was what I was doing. God works in mysterious ways.

Being so cautious about the traffic on the roads is not all I should have been looking out for. There are houses along the way with people looking out their windows. When I lit that cigarette miles back, someone happened to be looking out the window of their house. It's all at the moment, them looking out the window and me carefully lightin' my puff.

That moment and my praying-crying-for-help moment, I am forever grateful for. These two moments changed my life immensely for the better. Moments do change lives. Being a functioning alcoholic for years that fifth DUI was definitely heaven-sent. Today and forever I am thankful, grateful, and humble to the higher power of my understanding for taking me away from the toxic living death I was sentenced to because of my being an alcoholic.

If I a functioning alcoholic for years can recover from alcoholism you too can recover. I remained in a state of HOPE (hanging onto positive expectations) by immersing myself in recovery and becoming a student of sobriety (SOS 1). I was always in the ready, set, GO mode.

{G}ame

{O}n from one moment to the next. The recovery game was now my number 1 priority. 24-7. Recovery was life, and without it, living my using and abusing ways meant

{T}oxic

{D}eath. My unwavering daily conscious choices from one moment to the next were based on no TD for me. No toxic death for me. At least one AA meeting a day. Prayer and meditation all throughout the day. A self-help book here and there. Good AA fellowship was critical. Journalizing became a *way* of life. All my waking attention was focused on my newfound number 1 priority, staying sober. My TD lifestyle was put to rest.

> Do or do not.
> There is no try. (Yoda)

Along the way, I experienced a complete spiritual transformation. The psychic change is talked about in the *Big Book Doctors Opinion Story*. I surrendered to a new way to exist. If I can do this, you can too. I truly do wish you the best of luck.

Douglas M. Norgren

Student of Sobriety
SOS 1
KISS

It all started with an innocent KISS. Then came AA, LLD, SOS [1], and the rest.

{K}eep
{I}t
{S}imple,
{S}hithead.

I heard this acronym for the first time during my inpatient days and it struck a chord with me right from the get-go. Only four letters that triggered a lot of *sober-mind thoughts*. New sober spirit.

An innocent KISS. A new way to remember. Four letters to recall four words of remembering. I stood up and took notice the first time I heard "Keep It Simple, Shithead." I welcomed this way of saying and remembering things with open, hugging arms. Acronyms were foreign to me before this.

I am not a phone-text kind of guy, but I have been around that form of communication a little bit. To me acronyms and abbreviated words when texting are kind of like brothers and sisters. In a microwave, mindset society both are ways to communicate something fast and efficient. Both can be fun and less ho-hum than long-hand writing and remembering.

I have definitely had fun with the acronym KISS around the AA tables from the west coast to the east coast, and in the states of Minnesota and Wisconsin. Anyone can do the same adding drama by puckering up and blowing kisses to and fro. We are not allowed to be a glum lot, are we? Tough luck if no one cares for our antics.

KISS activated my infantile sober mind exponentially. ALCOHOLIC MIND thoughts rapidly became nonexistent, originally just triggering four words, and then came sentences and pages of related sober thinking, good sober thoughts unlike the toxic, poisonous ones of my drinking days. All is in our thinking, and KISS changed my drinking thinking to sober thinking forever. I became motivated and addicted from that first AA KISS. The next one that kept my sober mind stimulated and positive was AA.

AA

Alcoholics Anonymous has changed my life astronomically for the better, and it's God of my understanding's will to share this fact with people any chance I get. I owe my life to Alcoholics Anonymous.

Real early in sobriety, I needed my own acronym for AA to put a positive flavoring in my mouth, to negate my prior thoughts and feelings about Alcoholics Anonymous. Throughout my drinking career, I had laughed at the thought of AA. Joking with friends and smiling negatively to myself about such a cult. I needed my own AA acronym.

{A}ttitude

{A}djustment was the answer. Every meeting I attended, my attitude was miraculously more positive after the meeting than before it. During those early recovery days, acronyms were heard at the meetings and I began to birth many of my own.

HAH was one I heard at meetings many times.
{H}abits
{A}nd
{H}angouts. I needed new HAH in my life. New habits and new hangouts were essential for recovery. I started to learn new habits at my new number 1 hangout spot. The next AA Alano Club. I put down the drink and picked up the steps at these Alano Clubs.

{M}eeting
{M}akers
{M}ake it was something heard at many, many meetings. This had to be shortened to 3M. Meeting **m**akers **ma**ke it. All that is necessary in staying sober is to attend AA meetings: KISS. Ninety in ninety makes for a good start on a new way of life.

Attending AA meetings guarantees a
{W}inning
{E}dge to all. It's been said billions of times AA is a *we* program, a program of unity. All who are involved strive for the same goal: more sobriety. AA does give all the Winning Edge for more sobriety. HUGE WINNING EDGE mind food read at some AA meetings is *The Promises*.

God's Magic

My first Alcoholics Anonymous attitude adjustment home group always had what I wanted and yearned for in someone reading *The Promises*. This reading was the tune-up I needed to keep rolling down the road of recovery. I strongly encourage all to create a laser focus for their recovery by writing out this reading and carrying it with them wherever they go. It will adjust your attitude for the better. GM. Period.

{G}od's

{M}agic. Of course I needed an acronym for it. Below are God's magical words of *The Promises*.

If we are painstaking about this phase of our development, we will be amazed before we are halfway through. *We* are going to know a new freedom and a new happiness. We will not regret the past nor wish to shut the door on it. We will comprehend the word *serenity*, and we will know peace. No matter how far down the scale we have gone, we will see how our experience can benefit others. That feeling of uselessness and self-pity will disappear. We will lose interest in selfish things and gain interest in our fellows. Self-seeking will slip away. Our whole attitude and outlook on life will change. Fear of people and of economic insecurity will leave us. We will intuitively know how to handle situations that used to baffle us. We will suddenly realize that God is doing for us what we could not do for ourselves. Are these extravagant promises? We think not. They are being fulfilled among us, sometimes quickly, sometimes slowly. They will always materialize if we work for them.

The Promises reading is, without a doubt, the epitome of our acronym for hope. It keeps us hanging onto positive expectations for our future recovery. Eight times *we will* is used as a certainty for a positive personal change to occur in all of us, and *will* alone, five times. Alot of self-hype? We think not! These certainties adjust our attitudes toward the positive when we read and hear them. They are guarantees if we work for them. Fantastic attitude adjustment.

Now I had two AAs: Alcoholics Anonymous and Attitude Adjustment. Our attitudes are everything, and we tune them up with each and every hour of Alcoholics Anonymous. The meeting magic of each AA meeting, the positives, we soak up in that sixty minutes. PMA (Positive Mental Attitude) will always carry us further than a negative one. Writing about this stuff refreshes and revitalizes my spirit. Is anybody journalizing their AA meetings yet? There's more than one way to maintain a fit spiritual condition. Special note: our attitudes are everything.

Long before I attended my first AA meeting, I was involved with a business that was driven by self-hype, positive self-talk, positive self-affirmations, or whatever other label you want to tag on it. Whatever term floats your boat. Isn't the English language great? Three different ways to say the same thing, maybe a reason we Americans have so much trouble understanding each other. The abovementioned business taught me the importance of self-hype.

At any rate, with eight *we wills* and five *wills* embedded in *The Promises*, I hung onto God's will with all my sober mind's might. These *will* statements are certainties for a better life. They aren't maybes.

Early in sobriety, I was in no position to believe any of these promises, but because of that business I mentioned, I knew the power of *positive self-talk*. "Fake it till you make it" is one way to describe this magical power within all of us. Whether we realize it or not, we chatter to ourselves on and off. all day long. At times we may even raise our voices when self-talking.

Positive self-talk always leads to a better attitude than negative talking to ourselves. All will have a fitter spiritual condition after reading *The Promises*. These *AA promises* were the *Attitude Adjustment Seeds* I yearned to hear at each AA meeting for the first two years of my sobriety. These promises do become reality for all who work for them. One must believe and persist indefinitely with their recovery.

The Promises reading came to my rescue away from the AA tables during a trying monetary time in my life in a dramatic fashion. One personal promises story here is a must. At this particular time in my life, I needed this attitude adjustment to maintain my serenity and peace of mind.

About eighteen months into sobriety, I was seeking employment. I had a lot of applications out there, somewhere, but was not getting any calls to interview. My monies were dwindling. I was focusing my spending on just the necessities of the following: gas for the car, cigarettes, and tradition seven. The money I had in the bank was nearing ground zero soon. Anxious moments of concernment were becoming more and more the rule rather than the exception. My serenity and peace of mind were near extinction.

One morning at about three o'clock, I had to do my normal sleepwalk to take a leak. With more clarity than I can read it, I found myself reciting *The Promises* to the porcelain Gods. During my drinking days, my worship to the toilet was done a whole lot differently. Poisonous toxins usually spewed from my mouth while I was on my hands and knees holding unto the seat for dear life.

My unconscious promises early morning self-affirmation was the solution to regaining lost serenity and peace of mind. Fear of economic insecurity vanished when I woke for the day. What a miraculous late-night attitude adjustment.

About sixteen hours later that very same day, I went to an AA meeting. I was the last person getting there. One empty seat was left with about thirty people in attendance. I sat down, and there on the table was my savior, *The Promises* reading. Thirty people there, one minute before the hour, and no one cared to read *The Promises*:

These kinds of incidents blow me away. They put a smile on my face and a chill down my spine. Early in sobriety, I recall someone saying that coincidences are Godcidences. This kind of reasoning works for me. I have replaced the word *coincidence* with *Godcidence*.

God does work in mysterious ways. That early in the morning incident and the meeting later on in the day reaffirmed this fact again to me. A marvelous attitude adjustment times two. Both were brought on by great divine intervention. A one-two punch floored me back to no fear of *economic insecurity* as it is stated in *The Promises* reading. GM is what I like to call it. Not General Motors. God's Magic.

Related to GM and Godcidences, another acronym dropped in my lap at an AA meeting early in my sobriety days, GMC.

{G}od

{M}anufactures

{C}oincidences. I had heard before about him being a master weaver and working in mystical ways so I had no problem with GMC not being just a vehicle manufacturer. Being a professional SOS 1, I wrote this one down and never forgot about it.

GMC took my recovery life to another level. It reminded me about God and the fact that he makes no mistakes. All things happen for a reason. It reminds me how important acceptance is in our lives. Being a SOS 1, I thought about these kinds of things constantly as my acronym list grew and helped me more and more with each passing day of sobriety.

Sobriety had become a way of life. As a result of being a SOS 1, my mindset had changed from being a drunk to that of a sober soldier. A major shift in my thinking. Alcoholics Anonymous had now birthed into being my new TEAM.

{T}ogether

{E}veryone

{A}chieves

{M}ore. I heard around the tables of AA that recovery was a lifetime deal. That there is no graduating from this classroom. That if we want to keep living a life of recovery, we must continue to attend those meetings. The more we come together and share our very own experiences, strength, and hope, the more sobriety we each achieve. Has anyone ever heard, "We must give it away to keep it"? AA is the ultimate team for ALL involved to achieve more sobriety.

To attend an AA meeting takes a conscious choice on our part. I just kept making that choice one day at a time. I just kept making that conscious decision day after day. How about ninety in ninety as a goal? An assignment. Attend ninety meetings in ninety days. I assure you this will put a dent in your drinking thinking. If I can do this, you can too. Sobriety must be our number 1 priority till death do us part.

With sobriety being number 1 we must become a SOS 1 for survival's sake. It's natural for us to study the ways of Alcoholics Anonymous and especially pay close attention to the successful recovering alcoholics at the meetings we attend. Recovering means there is a lifetime contract here. Our nondrinking thinking must remain so for the rest of our lives.

Sobriety is a new way of life for us drunks which deserves our fullest attention. AA meetings are our classrooms for recovery which there is no graduating from. None of my formal schooling, including four years of college, had provided me with even one hour of study on how an alcoholic recovers from alcoholism. Inpatient and outpatient treatment programs are our introductory coursework for sober living, the foundation for a career of nondrink. Time spent in treatment is great and necessary, but there is so much more. Perseverance is required. Rarely does an alcoholic say that they are *recovered*. It's almost always stated *recovering alcoholic*. It's alcoholism, not alcoholwasm. Once an alcoholic, always an alcoholic. My outpatient counselor had *recovering alcoholic* in mind when she spoke of AA meetings.

She strongly urged the class to make AA a vital part of our lives till death do us part and highly recommended journalizing these hours. Before this, while going through treatment, I often wondered how they thought drunks could write so much. With all the step-work and accompanying other writing homework, how many English college majors did these counselors feel were in their presence? Now this journalizing suggestion. With all my formal education, including college, I really believed my extensive writing days were over. I roared to myself about that journalizing suggestion.

I don't know what came over me, but after my first AA meeting, I went home and started writing. Attitude adjustment blurbs I could remember from that hour were written. Sometimes only a sentence or two was written, in other instances, a page or more. The quantity was partially dependent on my LLD intake (Lotta Little Debbies). Cosmo brownies, Zebra cakes, Swiss rolls, and the rest. Being an attentive SOS 1, I pampered myself with sweets as this was the sort of thing recommended for our recovering venue.

I never held back on my Debbies. More often than not, I ate all in sight which was more than a couple times two. Journalizing and enjoying all my snacks, I came to the realization that sobriety really had become my number 1 priority. Without it, we have nothing. Our written out step one reminds us of that fact. Remember KISS? Why look any further. Sobriety must remain our number 1 priority. Forever and ever. Do or do not. There is no try. Just AI.

AI

{A}ccept

{I}it. When I read the abovementioned Yoda spiel and thought about it, I started to focus on not even using the word *try* any longer. Instead, words like *concentrate* and *focus* replaced it. Do we try to take a shower or focus on it and actually git er done? The below words of acceptance helped me focus on myself and my attitudes.

Acceptance is the answer to all my problems today. When I am disturbed, it is because I find some person place, thing, or situation—some fact of my life—unacceptable to me, and I can find no serenity until I can accept that person, place, thing, or situation as being exactly the way it is supposed to be at that moment. Nothing. Absolutely nothing happens in God's world by mistake. Until I could accept my alcoholism, I could not stay sober; unless I accept life completely on life's terms, I cannot be happy. I need to concentrate not so much on what needs to be changed in the world as on what needs to be changed in me and in my ATTITUDES.

With two letters, AI, life becomes totally different. First, we accepted that we were alcoholics. Then after finishing step 1, we accepted the fact that we were powerless over alcohol and that our lives had become unmanageable because of it.

After that, we must accept that a sober life takes work and life situations still come and go. The good and the bad. Life is just that. Ups and downs. Persons, places, things, and situations continually change and must be accepted.

To live life on life's terms we must change our thinking and attitudes towards these fluctuations, from our past stinking, drinking—thinking to new-found sober thoughts and attitudes. Our alcoholic minds must become sober. All AA meetings and readings help us to do just that.

Great new thoughts, habits, and directions are exposed to us at these meetings. Spirits to drown out that toxic alcoholic thinking of our living death days of the sip. I sip. I slip. I use. I lose. Today I choose not to lose. All is a choice. We must Accept It (AI), that being alcoholics requires a no-drinking attitude on our part.

When I see a Nike emblem, I am now reminded of accepting life on life's terms. Nike's playbook reads "Just Do It!" On the same note, ours must be "Just AI." Just accept it!

The Promises reading along with this AI reading provide great seeds for becoming an aspiring SOS 1. They are exceptional new spirits to lead the way for us all as we roll down the road of recovery. *The*

Promises is that self-talk/self-affirmation that all is a certainty with effort on our part, and the acceptance blurb in the *Big Book* reminds us that we can only change our attitudes and not the whole world around us. Extraordinary POM (Peace Of Mind) and serenity will prevail when both these seeds are taken to heart.

Just like *The Promises* reading, I strongly encourage all who are serious about their recovery to write out the acceptance words of knowledge. These two tools of the trade are the sharpest tools in the tool shed as far as I am concerned. Both make for good book marks and/or pocket reminders for the right attitudes toward which we should all strive toward. Our attitudes, our habitual thinking, are everything. POM and serenity will follow.

POM and serenity became my new addictions. Each day I yearned to go to another AA meeting for another shot of serenity accompanied by a POM chaser. Because of my journalizing of these meetings, my pink-cloud high lasted longer and was more intense in nature. I just AI and continued down the interstate of recovery.

Keeping AI in mind, DOA was next. I don't mean dead on arrival. With recovery being a *one-day-at-a-time* suggestion DOA is necessary.

{D}ay

{O}f

{A}cceptance. Acceptance of how our day unfolds. How persons, places, things, and situations change throughout our day. The flow of each day does not change the fact that we are alcoholics and can't even have one drink. Without recourse, we must accept the day's hand dealt to us.

If the fish aren't biting, maybe they will bite better tomorrow. If our mate/date don't have lovin' on their mind tonight, hopefully, tomorrow night. Maybe yesterday we planned on golfing, and today it's forty degrees with pouring rain. Sometimes our plans don't work out. This we must accept.

DOA reminds us that we are not in charge. Thy will, not my will, be done. One DOA at a time. The magic is in the HOW.

{H}onesty,

{O}penness,

{W}illingness. We must remain honest to ourselves, open to help, and willing to change. Our honesty is required in order to start recovering. RIGOROUS HONESTY is how it is stated in our *How It Works* reading. Admitting that we are powerless over alcohol and that our lives had become unmanageable is step 1. We had lives of lying and denying before fessing up to ourselves that we were self-destructive. Self-honesty starts our healing.

Our healing moves forward with an openness to a power greater than ourselves. Step 2: Came to believe that a power greater than ourselves could restore us to sanity. Open to the fact that we could not do this recovery thing on our own, and with a greater power than ourselves, sanity is possible.

Our willingness was necessary in step 3. We made a decision to turn our will and our lives over to the care of God as we understood him. His will, not our will, restores our sanity.

The word *decision* is the *key word* in step 3. What we decide on requires action on our part. Continual new behaviors. The rest of our lives must be lived with our step one self-honesty in mind. Along with our openness to a power greater than ourselves and the willingness to keep that *decision*, our guiding light. Just AI. One DOA at a time.

The HOW of recovery, steps 1 to 3, must remain a constant in our new sober mind for recovery to be a success. We must keep steps 1 to 3 in mind at all times. Just AI. They are the foundation for transforming our alcoholic minds into sober ones.

I don't know about you, but I diligently catered to my alcoholic mind for twenty-five plus years. The same perseverance is a must in recovery. We can't take this for granted or get complacent. We hear at AA meetings that there is no graduating from recovery or AA. The ancient school was that a person would go in for *the cure* and that our disease would disappear. Now called *treatment*, we have learned that this is only the beginning of our recovery from alcoholism. Step 10 gives us a clue that it is a lifetime deal by starting out with the word *Continued*. Continually focusing on the HOW, we must beware of HALT.

{H}ungry,

{A}ngry,

{L}onely,

{T}ired. During recovery, we must watch not to get too hungry. A liquid lunch must be a thing of the past. Extended happy hours are not a substitute for a suppertime meal. Our angry moments must be dealt with something other than the drink. Lonely moments can always be overcome with an AA meeting or a phone call to another recovering drunk. The right book will sometimes work. Tired thinking can lead to stinking thinking. The thought of just one drink cannot be tolerated.

With HOW, HALT, *Continued*, and the rest of ·step 10, our recovery lives now have some specific focus. Looking at steps 2 and 3 of the HOW, I realized that a power greater than ourselves in step 2 transitions to God in step 3 with a blink of an eye. Early in my sobriety, this God thing scared the hell out of me. I didn't consider myself very religious. I wondered how forgiving and punishing he may be.

God Times 3

Easing my mind of these fears I found out that there was always two less religious God's presence at all AA meetings. What else are meetings but a

{G}roup

{O}f

{D}runks. And if we are truly living a recovery program of our own, then we have

{G}ood

{O}rderly

{D}irection. I cringe when recovery people talk about working the steps. We can't just work them and forget they exist. We must incorporate them into our daily lives. We must always be motivated by the design for a living guide of the twelve steps. When we do then we are preceding in a good orderly direction.

When working in concert with the abovementioned GODs, I assure you will find a God of your own understanding. Working with a group of drunks in a good orderly direction for the rest of our lives, we do find a God of our own understanding. Working with a group of drunks in a good orderly direction for the rest of our lives, we do find a

{G}ood

{O}ld

{D}ude of our very own. Do or do not. There is no try. Do you want to live or do you want to die?

The twelve steps of Alcoholics Anonymous are definitely good orderly direction for any drunk to follow. Following the twelve-step design for living, we begin working on our old ego-driven ways.

Out with EGO, Work on EGI

An acronym for ego was brought to my attention during my first year of sobriety.

{E}dging

{G}od

{O}ut. What this means is staying true to our self-centered way of life rather than adapting to the twelve-step design for sanity becoming God-centered in the process.

During our cocktail days, we were ego-driven in all we did, and or, said. "I this" and "I that." I drank a magnum of vodka and smoked one-fourth ounce of weed with so and so last night. We ditched from the cops last night out in the country racing the back roads. I got lucky with Wanda Lust last night after a couple of shooters of tequila. Back in my college bartending days, I was a booty and bottle alcoholic who lived the catch and release program with the girls. My life was nothing but *I-centered* living death, totally egotistic in nature, no God in any of it. I was a servant to my EGO (Edging God Out), catering to my master, the sauce.

Looking back at it, I see where my drinking ego was replaced with AA's EGI. The rhetoric at AA meetings, their readings, and it's a twelve-step program put my ego to rest, little by little,

{E}dging

{G}od

{I}n. Mentioning some of these sources, I specifically point to the *Serenity Prayer* and again *The Promises* reading and the twelve steps. All have God and God of our understanding sprinkled throughout. The more we hear and say, the more it creeps into our being. Repetition with these sources leads to more and more of edging God in.

When we read the twelve steps and pray the Serenity Prayer, we are changing our alcoholic minds to a sober ones. Then we also hear that God assists our fellow AA people. God works through people at meetings. More EGI. How about the Lord's prayer at the end of the hour? More EGI. We are also taught to change from being self-centered to God-centered. More edging God in.

All of the abovementioned sources change our thinking, little by little, each time we read and hear them, changing our mindset from egoistic to God-driven, from toxic, poisonous thoughts to sober serene thinking. Each attitude adjustment hour we attend, we phase out our ego a little bit more and EGI naturally via all the "God this" and "God that." What happens is a reprogramming of our alcoholic mind to an others-based one. From a self-centered, destructive way of life to a God-centered, constructive, serving existence. A *psychic change*, like the *Big Book* mentions, takes place in us.

EGI ultimately leads to a complete PC. Not personal computer but

{P}sychic

{C}hange. This PC is the only cure we have as we are told in *The Doctor's Opinion* story at the beginning of the Alcoholics Anonymous *Big Book*.

I pondered on PC for a few years about what the hell it meant. Never being that English major at heart it took me a while. Staying persistent in my SOS 1 ways and keeping KISS in mind, I came to the conclusion that it meant a change in our thinking.

With this psychic change comes a newfound hope. I kept going to meetings for that serenity and POM that was present there. A majority of it because of *The Promises* and *Acceptance* readings. The more I read and heard these dialogues, the more I felt POM and serenity might possibly be God.

The Promises is GM. This reading assures us of a winning attitude and our attitudes are everything. Seeping into our minds with each reading of *The Promises* are all the certainties that will take place in our lives and the sentence "God will do for us what we can't do for ourselves" is more EGI. That blurb was the biggie for me. Where did my obsession, craving, and desire go? Like magic, gone—vanished.

With my want and need for alcohol gone, hoping for the rest of *The Promises* becoming reality was my prevailing attitude and all-encompassing spirit. Because of this newfound hope in life, I experienced a total spiritual transformation. More fuel for my sober thinking, sober spirit, was my calling. Besides my attitude adjustment hours (AA meetings), I began to work on my attitude with other sources. Working on one's attitude away from the tables of AA can only be a plus, right?

This newfound *hope attitude* we get from *The Promises* can be bolstered with positive self-help books. Why not dabble with this infant novel intoxication besides our AA meetings? Books assisted my normal run-of-the-mill recovery venue. Anything to maintain and bolster our spiritual condition, right?

During my drinking days, I was at it twenty-four hours a day. If I wasn't drinking I was thinking about drinking. An all-day, every day, ball and chain. Between my AA meetings and extra readings, I have never spent even half that time on a daily basis. Rapidly my alcoholic mind had been replaced by a sober mind which required less time and effort to maintain. If I can do this, you can do this.

The right books just fell into my lap from the skies above. When not even seeking another the next one appeared rearing their heads at rummage sales, flea markets, and even from my ex-girlfriends.

A newfound AA friend brought me the book *The Power of Now* by Eckhart Tolle.

Bill was my AA buddy's name. I had only been in his presence for a few AA meetings and fellowshipped with him for about twenty minutes after one of them. Bill said Eckhart and I share kindred spirits and that I would gobble up his book. That I did. God works in mysterious ways. All is God's country.

That Tolle book I strongly recommend to all people in recovery, and to all people in general who want to focus their lives on the moment at hand. The here and now. The present. Eckhart says the present moment is the field on which the game of life happens.

I personally ate and slept with that book for close to two years. It was a huge part of my morning meditation. It kept me in the one DOA at a time mode. Accepting each moment of the day with totality. No resistance and sweet surrender to God's will for that moment. How about a philosophical question here? How long is a moment?

In my years of research, I have come to my own conclusion that God is the moment. The moment is God. The here and now is God. With this in mind, accepting the moment totally leads to more POM and serenity. Therefore, for me, the longer I stay in the acceptance mode, the longer the moment is. I am an AAS man.

{A}ccept

{A}nd

{S}urrender man.

To go along with the books, for more sober mind food, I got my mitts on some recovery cassette tapes, not CDs. They were too modern for me. Cassette tapes. One of these was a Joyce Meyer beauty from my very first Celebrate Recovery Meeting after outpatient treatment. Again I was not patrolling this meeting for inspirational material other than the hour at hand. I was passing time before the meeting, looking at tapes displayed as I had a cassette player at the time. A free price tag and a catchy title were all it took. Maintenance of a fit spiritual condition can be addictive too.

What a gem, another needle in the haystack. The tape has slipped through my fingers, somewhere, and the name went with it. At any rate, Joyce went on and on about giving God glory, meaning to remain humble. God does for us what we cannot do for ourselves. Give God glory. Give thanks for all of our successes, and we will receive another. After listening to the tape mega times, another acronym was conceived.

{G}od

{G}ets

{G}lory. Triple *G*. God of our very own understanding did for us that which we could not do for ourselves. Humbly asking God to remove our character defects. Live and let God. With God all things are possible. Give God credit for all our victories, and there will be many more to come.

GGG. My confession of humility. All my victories are God-driven. I focus on not being the one running around snappin' my fingers and poppin' my bubble gum. With this in mind, I am also self-aware to the fact that I am not perfect. I realize my ego does shine through at times in the actions that I take. Spiritual progress rather than spiritual perfection is the target.

DIO and RWC

Remaining humble to a God of our understanding is a must. Our *confession of humility* should always be, "It's all God." Joyce says when we give God glory for our success, more will come. Give God credit for all our victories and more will follow.

{D}oubt

{I}s

{O}ut (DIO). We must have undying faith. Do we have it or not? We must remember, "Sometimes quickly, sometimes slowly." Successes will come if we work for them. God won't do our part but will do his. Success requires unwavering faith. DIO.

GGG in regard to beverage abstinence, "give GOD thanks each day," and it's a given you will remain alcohol-free. DIO. Being powerless over alcohol, "God did for us that which we could not do for ourselves." Staying humble in this fashion assures us more sober success, an extraordinary way of ridding ourselves of our ego. Constant humbleness to a power greater than ourselves.

A whole lotta GGG, and you will be RWG. Being humble and grateful for all assures us that we are RWG.

{R}ocking

{W}ith

{G}od. Rocking with a God of our very own understanding. With KISS in mind, God is any positive, and any negative is the devil, demotic, satanic.

RWG is getting into a flow, a rhythm of your very own in recovery, to abandon self-centeredness and become others-centered, to become God-centered. Each person's rhythm, RWG, is different. No two people should be the same. After all, a GOD of our understanding should be individualistic by nature, right?

Some people's only God is a Group Of Drunks. For others, God may be the Good Orderly Direction of the twelve steps.

With this in mind, it looks to me that there are at least God times two at all AA meetings. As long as we remain humble and grateful to some higher power, RWG is a certainty. RWG is the power source of our recovery. Our old egoistic ways were totally disharmonious with any power greater than ourselves. With ego comes insanity. EGO has been referred to as Edging God Out. We must EGI by getting and staying in rhythm with a God of our own understanding. RWG in order to continue recovering from a powerless and unmanageable existence of living death.

The step 3 prayer is a great tool to rid ourselves of EGO. With it, we become more and more God-centered in our ways… RWG.

Other tools of the trade are a part of our very own way of rockin' with God. Each of us is unique and differs on how much and how often we utilize a given tool. Each person may differ in how many meetings they attend per week? Which types and what times do they attend? How much sponsor time per week do they require? How much time is spent daily living step 11? Reach for God shots rather than liquor shots. Prayer and meditation shots are what the doctor orders. How much service work they do, and so on? Doing the next right thing is our compliance with RWG.

Of the tools we have at our disposal in recovery, step 11 will always be the one of greatest importance, and the more we utilize it, the more RWG. Improving our conscious contact with a God of our understanding, praying only for knowledge of his will for us and the power to carry that out. Looking at this KISS fashion, I take his will for us as the next right thing. Period.

For me, doing the next right thing, and concentrating on that conscious contact with my God, leads me to becoming my own best friend. My SOS 1 days remind me that this is a must for our recovery. RWG is living in harmony with God.

Recovery starts with hope and is made a lot easier RWG in harmony. After hope comes honesty accompanied by humility. Hope comes first. Then a whole lotta honesty. With that honesty comes humility, and the end goal must be harmony: hope, honesty, humility, and harmony, four *H*'s all in a row.

Our four *H*'s of recovery led me to realize I now must become a four *H*'er in order to keep recovering. Being an AA animal leads one to become a four *H*'er.

{H}ope,

{H}onesty,

{H}umility,

{H}armony. Quadruple *H* are spirits we must think about often. After thinking about these new-found spirits, they must be acted on. Four *H*-ing is the easiest, softest way to live a life of recovery. In RWG via step 11 and the other tools of our trade, the four *H*'s become our new way of life, living in a state of HOPE. Remaining honest to ourselves, others, and a God of our understanding. Truth does set us free. Be humble to the fact we can't do this recovery thing on· our own. It will take a power greater than ourselves. And lastly, that harmony with all is sanity/recovery.

Harmony with yourself, your God, and others is sanity. HIS.

{H}armony

{I}s

{S}anity. We must strive for harmony in all our relationships. Has anyone taken a drink or drug because of a poor relationship? Continual focus on the next right thing is a great way to ensure harmonious and saner lives.

Four *H*'s. All in a row. An orderly progression just like ABCD. A life of recovery it's as simple as A, B, C, and D. A ST/PC is all that is necessary. Our only cure. A change in our thinking from drinking thinking to sober thinking. Recovery is remaining in a sober mindset.

Now that we have identified the much-needed four *H* spirits we must concentrate on we are ready to move on to SOS 2 and SOMU.

Student of Spirituality
SOS 2
SOS 2 and SOMU

Becoming an SOS 1, we study and think about God of our understanding a lot. We find one that works for us and it becomes our God spirit.

Has anyone ever thought of spirituality of their understanding? I researched spirituality immensely in my first five years of soberness and needed an acronym to label it. SOMU.

{S}pirituality

{O}f

{M}y

{U}nderstanding. Still being an SOS 1 and RWG, there came a day when a little voice in my head, that conscious contact with God of my understandin' told me to look up the root word of spirituality, *spirit*, in the dictionary. Part of the definition of spirit said, "Something that moves us." Period. Add back the six letters of -*uality* to our root word and keeping KISS in mind, I deduced that SOMU was anything that moves me. I was looking for sober positives now rather than toxic, poisonous spirits that lead me to spiritual bankruptcy at the end of my boozing days.

Spirituality had frightened me before I cracked the dictionary that day. How spiritual must one be in order to stay sober? Maybe you have thought the same? Spirituality and religion seemed to always be on the same debate table.

Then to complicate matters, it is said that AA is a spiritual program. We must maintain a fit spiritual condition we are told in the *Big Book*. We must strive for spiritual progress rather than spiritual perfection.

How about spiritual transformation and spiritual awakening? Spiritual experiences. *Spiritual this* and *spiritual that*. Some spiritual this or that might be knocking at your head as you read this book. I laserly focused my attention on the abovementioned… something that moves us.

After looking up the word *spirit*, I realized I had now started to get my feet wet in becoming a

{S}tudent

{O}f

{S}pirituality (SOS 2). Along the way I was into the book *The Magic of Believing* by Claude Bristol, and on page 37, give or take, he refers to spirituality as being our thinking. This fits nicely with SOMU. KISS. Doesn't our thinking move us? We usually think before we act don't we? Some habits may not require much thought but most of our intentional behaviors do.

Being a totally focused SOS 2, now I began to dissect and tip upside down all spiritual this and that. Not being that English scholar, two big words in one sentence threw me for a loop. With spiritual transformation, I am now encountered with two big words strung together.

{S}piritual

{T}ransformation. It took me nearly eighteen months into soberness before I figured out what the word *transformation* meant. I blame it on not being a grammar geek. All I wanted back in my formal education days were questions of yes or no and a A–E options for their answers.

To KISS the meaning of transformation, I landed on the word *change*. Keeping with the word *change* and then adding to it spirituality being our thinking along with anything that moves us, I became aware of the simplicity that a ST could be. How about a cup of coffee right away in the morning? Every sip is a spirit. What about our morning shower? Every drop of water keeps me moving… more sober spirits. We use the spirits of soap and shampoo to go along with the drops of H_2O coming from our shower head. Some towel spirituality to dry off afterward. Back to some more Joe spirit sip. A whole lotta morning sober spirituality and breakfast hasn't even been conquered yet. Eggs and bacon definitely keep me moving!

Are you a golfer? Golfing is spirituality of my understandin'. When I get all four cheeks, the two I sit on and the two I smile with, into a golf shot, there is a whole lot to keep me moving. I wanna do it again and again. The sun is out and with a temperature of seventy-five degrees. Seventeen holes yet to play. Another three-plus hours of remaining in the here and now, beautiful landscaping and some wildlife along the way too. So many spirits in a round of golf. Spiritual bliss at its finest if not taken too seriously.

Maybe floating around in a boat fishing on a day like this is more your style. For sure more SOMU. Fish on. Grab the net. Gimme the net, I'll net it myself. You missed trying to scoop up my last fish. Land the fish. Take a picture of that lunker. Put it back in the lake or in the live well. All this action keeps me moving and ready for more.

How many spirits are there in landing a fish? We would all probably come up with a different number. Total spirit for the day. Sun spirit. Otherwise, the weather spirit may be one of thunder and lightning. The spirit of setting the hook. Ready for more fish spirit, like the battle to the boat. Takes the right-doing spirit in order to land it, the taking the picture spirit and so on, another kind of spirituality that is ingrained in the pleasure part of our life: SOMU.

Any pets kickin' around where you live? When Kissy Kitty comes strolling into the room, my spirituality is changed dramatically. At a given moment, she may transform my spirit from crying to smiling. Then there are the spirits of her purring and kitty talk. The spirit of her French kissin' my cheeks. Maybe a plop-down snuggle to my leg or chest is in order with this particular pop-in visit. I never know what kind of ST is in store for me when she makes my presence while lying in bed. Clawhickys are more welcomed with open arms when they don't draw any blood. Kissy Kitty can play cribbage with Barb and me as long as she doesn't start pegging for the other team. Pet spirituality is an extraordinary sober spirit for me. More SOMU.

How about the sport of sex when the sun doesn't shine or when it goes down? Kissie. Kissie. Huggin' and squeezin'! Mutually consented and shared climactic horizons. The touch of flesh moves us toward more. It keeps us thinking and moving.

Most must work in order to play. Our paycheck keeps us motivated to punch the time clock each day. Maybe a mate is our main incentive for working. Must pay to play.

SOMU tells me there are loads of different spirits to earn a paycheck. There are many different thoughts and actions before payday comes around. Tasks at work usually require thought and action to complete.

Our work day consists of tasks that must be accomplished. One task leads to another. Each activity leads us to the next all throughout our work day. One spirit. One task at a time. Work is spiritual whether we ever thought it was or not. There is always something moving us during our shift toward another payday in the near future.

Our work tasks, more often than not, require some thinking on our part. When keeping in mind the book, *The Magic of Believing*, explaining that our thinking is part of our spirituality, then we are faced with more spirituality embedded in our work.

So in summary, both thinking and something/ spirit that moves us (our next task at hand) are ingredients driving us each and every shift. SOMU therefore includes work.

With work, pleasure, and daily routine/necessary behaviors requiring spirit and spirits to follow through on, I came to the conclusion that life is spiritual.

{L}ife

{I}s

{S}piritual. Remember how concerned I was with the program of AA being a spiritual one. My

LIS perspective helped me ease my mind spiritually. I am not wanting to take anything away from the spiritual/religious tone here. In my mind, the spirit of all good things is the spirit of God.

Why all the hoopla about LIS? I thought spirituality could only be related to religion. Maybe you felt the same?

How is LIS related to our recovery then? Triple *S* is my answer. SSS.

{S}ober

{S}piritual

{S}implicity. I know I came into the program spiritually bankrupt looking to live on toxic bags, bottles, and cans spirits and now must strive to live on sober spirits. The name of the game is spirit.

Being a SOS 2 and keeping in mind SSS, I focused on any kind of sober spirit to continue down my road of recovery. Work and pleasure, done without the sip.

Back in our sippin'/using days, our spirit of choice lead us to spiritual bankruptcy. This spiritual base leads us to a TD way of life. I didn't want any more of that TD way of life. My toxic spirit of choice stopped moving me the way it initially did. Using and abusing lead me to rock bottom and a dire need for recovery.

In recovery, we are introduced to sober spirits which are all positive for a more fit emotional, physical, and spiritual way of life. I was in a state of PMS 1, when I concentrated on only sober spirits.

{P}erfecting

{M}y

{S}pirituality. PMS 1 became my way of life. I was always looking to the next source to enhance PMS 1, from the meetings I attended to the books I read, the time I spent praying and meditating, my fellowship with others and so on.

Spiritual transformations of sobriety rather than from liquids and chemicals were my gasoline to continue down the road to recovery. I sought out any form of sober spirit to keep my tank full. PMS 1 is always my end goal, spiritual progress rather than perfection. To KISS, in my mind, progress was staying sober. As long as I was staying sober, I was progressing. One sober DOA at a time.

Besides the concept of ST, I needed to keep with the KISS mode with the concept of fit spiritual condition. It needed to be softened up. Simplified. Sticking with spirituality being our thinking was the key. Incidentally, that fit nicely with hearing at AA meetings that we don't have a drinking problem, we have a thinking problem. We alcoholics think we can drink like normies, but we can't. Thinking we can is absolute insanity.

The driving force in all we do is our thinking. We must be aware of our thinking at all times. Do we have a pure thought strain of abstinence, or do we have too many thoughts of using still creeping into our minds now and again? Our alcoholic mind must be completely nonexistent.

How is your spiritual condition? Your mind-set? Your attitude? Your spirit? Your inner state? Not Highway 35 which you drive back and forth to work on. Our thinking could be used for any of these questions. Our English language is great, isn't it? Many different words with similar meanings. Maybe this explains some craziness in people.

A fit spiritual condition in regard to a recovering alcoholic is sober spirited thoughts rather than alcoholic minded thoughts. This requires our attitude to remain nonalcoholic. Our attitudes are everything, and we do have a choice in determining the flavoring ours. The spirit of the letter *T* is the key to a fit spiritual condition.

To maintain a fit spiritual condition in regard to the sip, it comes down to the letter *t*. Our overall spirit must be transformed from an "I can drink" to an "I can't drink." Throughout our drinking days, we kidded ourselves many times that we could drink normally, lying and denying along the way. Being an alcoholic, we must just add the letter *t* to the word *can*. When we find ourselves saying to ourselves, we can drink normally.

SOT

{S}pirit

{O}f

{*T*} is where the rubber meets the road in our recovery. Our self-talk must be that of saying to ourselves that we can't drink instead of lying to ourselves that we can drink. Anytime the thought of a sip crosses our mind, we must discipline our thoughts back to we can't drink. Any doubters here? How about step 1?

Step 1 of Alcoholics Anonymous says we admitted we were powerless over alcohol and that our lives had become unmanageable. This reminds me that alcohol is nothing but trouble. SOT. *T* plus six letters added to it is what happens when we alcoholics mess with the drink. Trouble as we found out the first time working step 1. This particular SOT is what we want to put behind us.

Getting back to living the steps rather than working them lets focus on living step 1 in order to avoid trouble. All who truly want recovery should seriously consider personalizing step 1. Live step 1 by writing it out to say "I am powerless over alcohol, and my life becomes unmanageable when I drink." Write it out more than once, and this one sentence can be used for a daily reflection bookmarker and personal pocket cue card for starters. Both would make for excellent reminders of the fact that alcohol is trouble for us alcoholics. Having these reminders at our fingertips is a great example of living the steps.

Both of the above phrases are extraordinary tools to add to our tool shed for recovery. I can't drink, and our personalized step 1 sentence are fantastic self-affirmations that must be incorporated into our daily self-talk. The word *can't* is a one-word ST away from the drink, and our personalized step 1 sentence tells us what happens when we give in to the "I can drink attitude."

Trouble always rears its head when we think we can take a drink. Rigorous self-honesty is required always.

Following through on my SOS 2 train of thought, I realized one word can be highly spiritual in nature. Along the way, I even heard that JESUS was known for saying that his words are spirits. Because of this I felt compelled to add another *S* to my original KISS acronym.

KISS,S

KISS with three *S*'s.
{K}eep
{I}t
{S}imple
{S}hithead,
{S}pirituality. A smooch with three *S*'s was now my all and encompassing way of softening up spirituality. Spirituality was now anything from one word to a whole Bible's worth of spirituality and anything/ everything in between. There is bliss in KISS,S. What a game-changer.

Triple *S* was born rapidly after the birth of KISS,S during my SOS 2 days of heavy research and contemplative thought.
{S}ober
{S}piritual
{S}implicity shed unlimited spiritual light and simplicity power to SOMU. Having to do with recovery, I realized that spiritual simplicity is as simple as sober spirits or using spirits. That's all I needed to be con-

cerned with. Choose one, and I will continue to recover. Choose the drink, and trouble and/or death is nearby. Just what I was looking for—sober spiritual simplicity.

Speaking of a mystical Godcidence sober spirit, I'd like to share another eye-opener I had the other day. It was on my way to town to do some errands. My radio station was on my go-to political channel. The announcers were talking about our mental health in regard to dealing with our current once in a hundred years pandemic. Another light bulb came on in my head.

Years back, I had meditated on the term mental health. I can vividly remember telling myself and a few AAers that spiritual condition and mental health could be used interchangeably. Spiritual and mental can both be described as our thinking. Health and condition could be interchanged. This Godcidence was definitely a sign/omen that day.

How about changing the radio from a political channel to one with music? Another ST at the touch of our fingertips. SSS. Political spirit to musical spirituality.

Early on in my soberness, it knocked me in the noodle one day how uplifting the right music can be. I was brought up on fifties, sixties, and seventies lovey dovey genre. Kissie, kissie. Lovey dovey. Stand in one spot, and whirl it around a lot. Buddy Holly, Elvis Presley, Beatles, Beach Boys, and all the rest.

This type of music always puts a smile on my face and a bounce to my booty. I realized I could drown out any stinkin', drinkin', thinkin', or a negative attitude of any fashion that starts to hinder my spirit with my music of choice. I could SAS any negative thought strain away.

{S}ing

{A}nd

{S}mile. We can always tune into our favorite radio station or whatever kind of music medium is at our disposal and SAS our dismal mindset away. There haven't been many times that when I started to sing along with my fav's that a smile on my face wasn't far behind, another instant attitude adjustment. A self-chosen action on our part to drown out any negatives in our spirit. Dick Van Dyke in his ninetieth birthday interview on the Access TV show insisted that a major key to his longevity was song and dance.

The type of music is what I want to shine a light on now. Listening to music affects our thinking and ultimately our prevailing attitudes. Listening to sad songs will make us sad. Listening to hard-core rap will get us in a rammy frame of mind. Songs of cheating will get us thinking about cheating. Music of our drinking days could very well trigger thoughts of our partying ways. We must be mindful of our musical selections.

Some may reach for a drink when they get sad. A rambunctious mood may lead some to drink. Others reminded of their cheating ways may pour a drink to forget their infidelities. We must stay away from GIGO. Beware: music does affect our mood.

Stay Away from GIGO

{G}arbage

{I}n,

{G}arbage

{O}ut. We are now aware of the fact that our thinking affects our actions. If we feed our minds with negatives, garbage enters, and then our actions, more often than not, will be accompanied by negative coloring. Garbage behaviors of anger, guilt, cheating, and drinking must become a thing of the past. Our music selections can trigger these ugly outbursts. A fit spiritual condition requires us to always be seeking the next right thing. It's tough to come up with the next right thing when we are feeding our minds with garbage.

Because a fit spiritual condition must be maintained in order for us to keep rollin' down the road of recovery I came up with another acronym to keep me on the straight and narrow. Triple *N*.

{N}o

{N}egative

{N}ature. Triple *N* was the laser focus for me looking to PMS 1 throughout my early years of sobriety. I now see that the word *nature* could very well be replaced with the word *spirit*. To keep with KISS mindset, a sober spirit-based life was anything that was positive in nature. Triple *N* became a thought discipline of mine. No GIGO for me. We alcoholics must stay on the up and up. Always the positive in mind. The next right thing.

NNN is an extraordinary spiritual condition to progress toward always looking to turn negatives into positives, searching for the good in all, always seeing the glass half full rather than half empty. We are not getting older. We are becoming more experienced. How about SAS when we become down and out? Sing and smile.

Triple *N*. No GIGO for me. Turn a negative into a positive. These were my attitudes after I had a one-on-one sit-down with my outpatient counselor in her office, eyeball to eyeball sitting at her desk.

I was there for my weekly conversation about my recovery progress. However she brought it up and whatever intentions she had for doing so, she proceeded to tell me that 999 out of 1,000 people who attend out-patient will be back for more. That day I went home and wrote out the sentence: "I am one in a million." I tacked that reminder right above my bedroom light switch. A whole lotta do or do not, there is no try. I am in it, to win it.

I also applied my NNN to what parts of the *Big Book* were useful to me. In the back of the book are people's stories. I cared not to read them much as a lot of them talked about slipping. The mention of slipping was garbage to my mental health and served no purpose in PMS 1. Perfecting my spirituality did not include reading the word *slip* over and over again. What we read does affect our thinking. If we don't read the word *slip* over and over again, we are less apt to think about it. Just like the word *try*, I consciously avoided giving the word *slip* any daylight.

My philosophy on these personal *Big Book* stories helped a thirty-year pin veteran one afternoon at an AA meeting. At a noon meeting of about twenty people, while sharing, he wondered out loud why his nine-month sponsee was questioning him about slipping. The sponsee had asked him about the timing of a slip. Was it a good time to do so after nine months of sobriety? The vet was curious as to why he had to entertain such a question.

After the meeting, I gave him the answer to his question. I brought it to his attention how much slipping was embedded in the stories part of the *Big Book*. Asked him if his sponsee read these stories religiously. A lot of sponsors recommend reading one story before turning in for the night. Guess what, what we concentrate on before bed is what our mind works on all night long. There's no wonder why someone thinks about slipping when they program their mind right before bed that it's part of the path to recovery. My listener that day could have swallowed up hordes of insects as his jaw dropped when pointing out the above. Caution. Reading does affect our thinking.

SLIP

My acronym for SLIP is
{S}pirituality
{L}osing
{I}ts
{P}riority. Spirituality, our thinking, must be priority 1. A fit spiritual condition requires our fullest attention.

What are we thinking about? Do we have thoughts of a sip? That alcoholic mind creeping in? We can't have one ass cheek sitting on a bar stool downtown and the other on an AA chair. Our sober mind must remain totally focused via thought discipline. We can change our thinking at any given moment with a conscious choice to do.

Just like the GIGO *Big Book* stories I chose to run from, I consciously made the choice to incorporate step 11 into my daily regimen. Become your own best friend by living step 11 rather than just working it, praying and meditating daily. Boy does that do wonders for one's mental health. Utilizing step 11 throughout the entire day will help with GIGO and keep us on the path of triple *N* living.

PAD and PUSH when needed.
{P}ray
{A}ll
{D}ay. Pray all day with all your concerns and moments of thankfulness, whenever they pop you in the noodle. Forgiveness, direct amends, divine guidance, and gratitude prayers are some examples of a

conscious connection with our God that can be done effectively throughout our day. PAD does enhance our spiritual condition.

Some have called the above prayers microwave prayers. PAD can include GGG and RWG conversations with our very own personal God. Short prayers of "Thy will be done" and "Thank you, God" always help to keep out the garbage. To go about your day with God-consciousness always makes for a better ride.

If you mean business with this recovery way of life, let no one or nothing stand in your way. When a thought that requires prayer crosses your mind, pray. Take a quick moment wherever you are and whatever you are doing at the time.

One time in Victorville, California, at about the time of the mid-day rush hour, I felt the need to bow my head in prayer while waiting at a red light. Before I could say my *amens*, horns were honking, and fingers were flying. No blue flashing lights though. I made the green light the first time around and proceeded on my way in a miraculously serene fashion waving as I drove off down the road. No harm. No foul.

God of my understandin' isn't fussy about when and where I pray. As long as I acknowledge his presence and I am sincere in my heart, my spiritual connection is a success. I bet God of your understandin' isn't that picky either on when you reach out in your moment of prayer. I heard once that you don't even need to worry about the clothes you have or don't have on.

GOMU

{G}od
{O}f
{M}y
{U}nderstanding has never rejected me when reaching out to him while sitting on the toilet. If I mind my manners all is okay. If the thought of prayer enters my mind I hold nothing back. A holy shit sit I have done on more than one occasion. When I feel a need to pray when sitting on the toilet, I do just that. GOMU does not expect me to be dressed for the prom and in a kneeling position every time I wish to speak. Rapping while crapping is okay.

Another go-to microwave prayer environment of mine is at the gas pump. Just like in the bathroom, my prayer of thanks, or whatever it may be, does not happen every time I fill my tank. My microwave prayer of thanks at the filling station is sometimes nonverbal. I point to the spirit in the sky and thoughts of another full tank are on my mind. After a point to the sky, a thumbs up to GOMU is next. He knows all my thoughts so that is all that is needed. Entertainers and athletes point to the sky here and there. How about you and me doing the same? All prayers of humility and appreciation will upgrade your spiritual condition. Your mental health will soar.

Sometimes and some things require prayer to be PUSH rather than microwave in nature. We must

{P}ray

{U}ntil

{S}omething

{H}appens. Jerry Savelle in his book *Expect the Extraordinary* suggests a great way to PUSH. He talks of doing so in an affirmative fashion, to thank God for working *behind the scene* on our prayer requests until they are answered. Give God a prayer of thanks along the way before we see the ultimate answer. PUSH.

Some things we pray for take longer than others. PUSH. Sometimes quickly, sometimes slowly. PUSH. All is on our creator's watch, not ours. Keep the faith. DIO. Our psychological state of mind must not include failure as an option.

An example of a PUSH prayer is going through an illness or injury. Maybe the injury of a broken bone confronts us. After we have prayed for God to assist our doctors and nurses throughout, there is the recovery time of the injury. A prayer here and there throughout the day till complete recovery is huge. Praying for a speedy recovery and absolute success. Being thankful, grateful, and humbled that God is working behind the scenes to ensure us a successful return to normal. PUSH. Keep praying affirmatively until complete recovery.

How about our alcohol illness/disease? We may have to pray in our search for the right sponsor. How about living the steps prayers? There are always the prayers for doing the next right thing. Maybe prayers to which meetings we should attend if given a choice? Pray affirmatively for cravings for alcohol to become nonexistent in our minds. The list of PUSH prayers throughout our recovery lives is endless. Both PUSH and PAD will enhance our chances of living a life of sobriety.

Living step 11 is magical. Step 11 encourages us to practice prayer, to continue talking to God of our very own understanding daily, even when it seems like a senseless activity. My God does come toward me when I seek him.

I find prayer to be an exercise of the soul. A single prayer is never useless or wasted. I always come away from prayer time feeling better about everything.

Waiting and anticipating responses to our prayers takes patience. Sometimes quickly, sometimes slowly but we have our job to do also. Our job is to do the footwork and to trust. Faith without works is notta. Wanted outcomes will always materialize if we work for them. Spiritual discipline with both our conscious contact with our God and our effort is required.

Both our physical actions and our mental aspect of praying are required for sustaining a fit spiritual condition. PUSH and PAD both mental aspects help us to keep progressing spiritually. After all, aren't we seeking spiritual progress rather than spiritual perfection?

Our very own spiritual discipline must drive us onward down the road of recovering. Spiritual discipline rewards us with sobriety, a positive inner state, and a saner lifestyle. Discipline with absolutely no complacency is required. To avoid SLIP, repetition of things that keep us in the flow of our program must be continued indefinitely. With repetition comes newfound sober habits. These habits must accompany us to our graves.

To ensure SLIP does not occur, we can keep in mind, "one day at a time." We know that certain things should be done daily. Each of us must find a personal flow or rhythm of our very own. Morning mediation, and for how long? How many AA meetings do we attend a week? How often do we talk with our sponsors and sponsees? The service work we get involved with. Time spent in step eleven and so on. Living step 11 and the rest help us to keep on track for a sober life. Nothing but positive advances towards more sobriety.

Keeping positive in spirit will enhance our chances of not having a slip. In regard to sobriety, any drinking thoughts would be negative and non-drinking would be positive. The twelve steps of Alcoholics Anonymous help us stay on the up and up with ourselves, a God of our understanding, and other people. They keep us in a sober frame of mind rather than a drinking one. Living these steps instead of working on them is a fantastic spiritual discipline. This discipline does lead to spiritual progress.

All these steps contribute to our spirit of recovery. We must keep our alcoholic minds in check with new sober spirits. Our new sober thinking and attitudes must always be the predominant *inner state* we now live by.

Keeping our spirit refreshed and revitalized is that rhythm of our very own program of recovery. NNN is what we must strive for. Positive self-talk is where it's at. There are some superb bits and pieces of self-talk statements peppered throughout the *Big Book*.

Page 32 of the *Big Book* has a dandy on it. We absolutely insist on enjoying life. NNN in that sentence.

How about the second paragraph of the long version of the Serenity Prayer for keeping to our NNN spiritual progress? Living one day at a time. Enjoying one moment at a time. Enjoying sounds like a positive spirit to me. Enjoying is our spirit just as well as the *we will* statements of *The Promises*. There is no negative nature in either.

Remember the one in a million flash card I had above my bedroom light switch? Norman Vincent Peale in his book *The Power of Positive Thinking* upgraded that one tremendously when he strung together the two words *spiritual millionaire*. Holy shit did that hit home for me.

During my days of being an avid SOS 2, I learned that spirituality was our thinking. If we replace spiritual with the word *thinking*, a thinking millionaire is the result. I took that to the bank and ran with it. Lots and lots of compounding spiritual thoughts and corresponding actions.

How about maintaining a fit spiritual condition relating to being a spiritual millionaire? Now NNN meant being a spiritual millionaire. RWG meant being a spiritual millionaire. The next right thing fits in. Triple *G* fits into padding my spiritual bank account. I self-talked to myself for a good period of time that I was a spiritual millionaire. DIO.

Peale also writes in the abovementioned book how earth-shattering the two words *I* and *believe* can be. Say these two words to ourselves three times in a row. I didn't stop with just three. I believe. I believe. I believe. Always ST for the better.

Another invincible self-talk I heard around the AA tables was "I get to" rather than "I got to." Another one-letter ST. Changing the *o* to *e* in the word *got*. Focus on jumping out of bed in the morning and telling yourself "I get to do this, that, and the other today." Use it throughout the day. Something like the next thing I get to do is... Your day will go better. You might even walk around with a smile on your face all day.

A positive *spirit or attitude* is what we are striving toward at all times in order to maintain a fit spiritual condition. NNN. Rather than negative self-talk, we must maintain positive self-talk, anything that works to combat intruding negative mind warfare. Saying something to yourself over and over again your thinking, your attitude, and then your spirit becomes positive again. Our attitudes are everything when concentrating on a fit spiritual condition.

With AA being a spiritual program in which we strive toward progress, maintaining a fit thinking condition rewards us with success. Repetition of our positive self-talks keeps us progressing toward more and more sobriety time. With repetition comes new-found sober habits.

Back to the habit of GGG affirmative microwave prayers throughout the day. GOMU brought it to my attention that these were amazing blurbs of self-talk. When God speaks, I do not argue with him. Positive prayers equal positive self-talk.

FAITH

Maintenance of a fit spiritual condition requires thinking discipline. Staying on the positive. We must keep the faith. Always remember

{F}antastic

{A}dventures

{I}n

{T}rusting

{H}im. There is no room for doubt. DIO.

As the Bible says faith comes from hearing not from having heard. In one ear and out the other sound familiar? We must hear something over and over again before it sinks in.

Faith brings me back to GM. *The Promises* reading. When you trust in him all the promises, all the adventures do come true. We have heard it time and time again around the AA tables of the world.

Meditation became an integral piece of my faith. Meditating on each sentence of *The Promises* will bolster your faith. Want faster results, change the *we*s in each sentence to *I*'s. Excellent self-talk will emerge.

PMS 1 (**p**erfecting **my** **s**pirituality) was the driving force throughout my intense SOS 2 days. I was concerned with how spiritual/religious I must become in order to continue recovery. Researching and pondering on that research led me to thoughts of how simple spirituality can be. Hence, SOMU.

The word *meditation* was the embryo, the lynchpin for me to transform from being a SOS 2 pupil to becoming a SOS 3.

{P}rotecting

{M}y

{S}anity was the driving force propelling my studies of sanity. PMS 2.

Student of Sanity
SOS 3

With insanity in mind, and the twelve steps our foundation to restore sanity in our lives, SOS 3 came naturally to me.

{S}tudent

{O}f

{S}anity. I had come to realize POM and serenity, a great spiritual condition to live life are natural inner states of our being when we make sane decisions rather than insane ones, A1. There is always less collateral damage if there is any at all. Fewer people were hurt, if any. Less money is spent on unnecessary things. Less time fixing wrong decisions. And the list goes on.

With a whole lotta PISSS (**power in sober spiritual** simplicity) still in my pants from my intense SOS 2 days, I leaned into the word *meditation*. Just like the word *spiritual*, it was frightening to me at first glance. A light bulb came on to look up the word *meditate* in the dictionary. Part of the definition was the two words: *contemplative thought*.

Contemplative thinking fit right in with SOMU. I had already come to the conclusion that a major part of spirituality is thought. Pause or ponder could even be injected into the definition of meditation.

These different words to describe meditation simplified my program astronomically. Before cracking the dictionary that day, I had thoughts of sitting in a corner somewhere with my head down muttering to myself as being the only way to meditate. My studies of meditation brought it to my attention that there is no wrong or right way to meditate. In regard to meditation, the only way you can screw it up is if you don't do it at all. One author brought it to my attention that meditation is a great way to become your own best friend. KISS. Now meditation is one of my own making.

MIA

Keeping with the words contemplative thought at the forefront of my mind, MIA was birthed. Not missing in action, instead

{M}editation

{I}n

{A}ction. MIA I go about my day.

MIA. Think before you leap. Respond to a situation rather than react. Meditate, pause, and ponder any situation we encounter. A *response* rather than a *reaction* is always saner. There is no contemplative thought in reacting.

Say we go to the doctor, and they prescribe some type of medication for our condition. After a few days of being on the prescription, we would want to be responding rather than reacting to it. Reacting to it would mean it's detrimental to our well-being and responding to it would signal a positive direction in improving our condition. Responding to something is always positive and reacting is negative.

If the negative constitutes insanity, and the positive is sanity, then MIA leads to saner responses to all our life situations. If we pause, ponder, or meditate on all and go with the positive that comes to mind, then our sanity is restored in all we do. This relates to doing the next right thing or the next best thing which is taught in AA. Positive direction is the spiritual progress that is necessary for us to continue recovering.

MIA…responding rather than reacting is our path to sanity. We live in a microwave reactionary society. I learned that responding to life rather than reacting helped PMS 2. Eckart Tolle says our society is a mass of collective insanity. I myself have often meditated on facts such as people making love to their text machines, driving down the road with mood-altering music playing, talking to their passengers, and all the while making decisions that may be of great importance. If these automobile drivers are of the female persuasion, powdering their noses left-handed with their man's hands on her legs could also be thrown into this insane mix of complete stimulus overload. These decisions are in a reactionary mode rather than in a meditative responsive fashion. Remembering our doctor's prescription example, reactions are negative, and responses are positive.

The portrait above of some drivers in America today points to the fact of insanity-based decisions today that lead them to an insane way of life rather than that of a saner existence. These insane decisions lead to more insanity in our lives. More drama. Has anybody ever taken a drink or drug to deal with the drama in their life? A whole lotta unneeded bull shit happens when we react to life rather than respond.

PS not BS

PS rather than BS is the easier, softer way to live.

{P}recious

{S}anity. If sanity is what we are seeking, our decision should be based on only the relevant stimuli to that decision. Contemplative thought is required for a more serene, dramaless decision. Less drama equals more serenity and sanity.

I can't see all the decisions one makes along that drive to Disneyland while accompanied by vast amounts and forms of stimuli at once could be anything other than reactions rather than responses. Total BS. Insanity and chaos are attached to any reaction. Serenity and POM cannot be at a very high level.

MIA is the healthy heartbeat toward good mental health. Laser focus in the MIA way is a blow torch that ignites Perfecting My Spirituality (PMS 1) and with that comes Protecting My Sanity (PMS 2). Total mindfulness when making decisions leads to more sanity/serenity. MIA I go about my day.

Sticking with the word *serenity*, an excellent weapon we can use to help us through trying decisions is the Serenity Prayer. Saying it to ourselves and contemplating it will help us enormously. Looking at it now it reads as follows:

God, grant me the serenity to accept the things I cannot change, the courage to change the things I can, and the wisdom to know the difference.

During my SOS 1 days, I learned that the three keywords in the Serenity Prayer are *accept*, *courage*, and *wisdom*. Concentrating on these words does lead to saner choices.

Focusing on accept must be first and foremost. Remember AI? Lack of acceptance has been the cause of all our problems according to the Alcoholics Anonymous *Big Book*.

I believe the biggest whoop-de-do to contemplate on as far as acceptance goes is on page 417 of the *Big Book*. These words of wisdom I brought to your attention in the SOS 1 section of this book but can't be studied enough. In all my travels, my AA home group in Cloquet, Minnesota, was the only huddle house that read it religiously before each meeting along with the Preamble, *How It Works*, and the rest. Now I see there are fancy rainbow-colored *acceptance* wallet cards for sale on the internet. Below is how the *acceptance* wallet card reads.

Acceptance

And acceptance is the answer to all my problems today. When I am disturbed, it is because I find some person, place, thing, or situation—some fact of my life unacceptable to me, and I can find no serenity until I accept that person, place, thing, or situation as being exactly the way it is supposed to be at this moment. Nothing, absolutely nothing, happens in God's world by mistake. Until I could accept my alcoholism, I could not stay sober; unless I accept life completely on life's terms, I cannot be happy. I need to concentrate not so much on what needs to be changed in the world as on what needs to be changed in me and my attitudes.

Alcoholics Anonymous Page 417

Back to my home group reading of acceptance. It ended a little differently. It ended with the sentence, "Live in the solution, not the problem." The solution is our program for recovery.

Keeping this last sentence in mind until I could accept my alcoholism, I could not stay sober, living step 1 seems to be a must. We must maintain this mindset forever and ever. Remembering our "I can't" drink self-talk, rather "I can" is living step 1. Then there's the personalized step 1 bookmark we can also glance at for a reminder.

What needs to be changed in me and in my attitudes reminds us that our attitudes are everything. Attitudes are our habitual thinking. Self-talks like the above help create habitual thinking which ultimately becomes our prevailing attitude that drinking only results in BS rather than PS.

Time now to put our thinking cap on and turn to the second major word in the Serenity Prayer. Courage. Cracking the dictionary again I came across the words *grit, guts, heart, nerve, spunk, backbone, boldness, resolution, dauntlessness, daring,* and even the word *SPIRIT.*

The courage to change the things I can. Live in the solution, not the problem. Do you have the guts to say no to a drink offer? Do you have the spirit to say no? How about the backbone and spunk to live a life of recovery instead of one of using and abusing? Do you have the grit to shy away from any triggers which may lead to a drink? We can all change our spirit of drinking to that of not drinking. It's all in our choice at any given moment. The decision not to take a drink.

Now to the third golden nugget word of the Serenity Prayer—*wisdom.* Words like *insight, science, judgment, learning, knowledge, information,* and *common sense* were used to explain *wisdom* in my dictionary.

I personally need not look any further than my own common sense related to taking that first drink. Years of accumulated past drinking information results in self-knowledge which gives me the insight, that one drink leads to never having enough to drink.

In the past, one drink leads to never enough. One on my end table near my bed at night and sometimes more under the bed. I have the wisdom to know that I can't even take one drink. That experiment has been rehearsed more than enough times.

The Serenity Prayer is a fantastic *go-to* for coping with each and every day. Each and every trying moment in a given day. The three golden nugget words of *accept, courage*, and *wisdom* give great clues for a responsive life rather than reacting to choices that must be made. Use of the Serenity Prayer throughout the day is MIA at its finest. Far more PS than BS.

All of us know that BS stands for bullshit and that bullshit is something we care not to experience. PS is totally living in the here and now with POM and Serenity paving the way in all we do and encounter. With PS, there is never any accompanying BS.

In regard to our drinking days, maybe the only precious sanity we ever experienced was when we passed out? We were always chasing and consuming our sips in hopes of attaining PS. With each sip we took the BS piled higher and higher. Our living death sipping ways were totally insane and what we did to get and consume our beverage was anything close to sanity. There was so much lying, denying, and collateral damage involved with our toxic ways. For me, all that went with my drinking was total bullshit with no precious sanity or serenity. You can recall your own insane ways with the drink and decide for yourself on the BS vs. PS issue.

Our written out step 1 reveals the BS which accompanied our slamming and jamming ways. Step 1 brings to light our insane ways due to our alcoholic lifestyle. It shows the unnecessary drama and chaos involved with pursuing a career in poisonous spirit consumption: total BULLSHIT with eight capital letters.

Active recovery does lead to precious sanity and stillness of mind. In recovery, we make saner decisions as we are not being guided by our alcoholic minds. There is a whole lot less hoopla in our lives. Doing the next right thing will always be accompanied by PS. To attain more and more PS, we must

{S}urrender

{T}o

{T}he

{M}oment each step of the way with no mind chatter of the past or future. That PM (**p**resent **m**oment) must be free from personal stimuli overload. Personal stimuli overload is too many things coming at us at once that affect our doing and deciding to do things without much thought. Become friendly with the moment. We must have complete PM awareness to one decision at a time.

I realize it's an ATM planet out there, but ITM is what I learned to concentrate on when looking toward more sanity and a fitter spiritual condition.

{I}n

{T}he

{M}oment is where the game of life is played. The here and now. PS is the ultimate payout when living ITM. ITM keeps us from losing ourselves in

the world or in our own minds. We can't allow ourselves to get lost in either.

Step 11 is huge for living ITM. To PAD,
PUSH, and MIA along the way. To keep the faith
remember DIO, and there are Fantastic Adventures
In Trusting Him. Special note: read *The Promises* at
any time to keep the doubt out. Besides the affirmative prayers and others mentioned so far, the biggest
whoop-de-do of them all for me to pray on is the AA
Preamble. Let's look at it now.

AA Preamble

Alcoholics Anonymous is a
fellowship of men and women
who share their experience,
strength, and hope with each
other that they may solve their
common problem and help others to recover from alcoholism.
The only requirement for membership is a desire to stop drinking. There are no dues or fees for
AA membership; we are self-sup-
porting through our own con-
tributions. AA is not allied with
any sect, denomination, politics,
organization, or institution; does
not wish to engage in any con-
troversy, neither endorses nor
opposes any causes. Our primary

purpose is to stay sober and help
other alcoholics to achieve sobriety.

ESH

{E}xperience

{S}trength

{H}ope for others is a great premise on what we
can pray for. After all, our primary purpose is to stay
sober and help other alcoholics do the same. Praying
for the insight and guidance to help our brothers and
sisters helps keep us on the others-centered channel
instead of our old ego-driven ways. A whole lotta
give it away to keep it. Live in the solution, not the
problem.

I passionately utilize the Preamble in my walk
with recovery. I have prayed for ESH throughout
recovery and even on a bone-chilling, cold, subzero-
mile-and-half walk to a meeting. Going to any length
maybe?

That six months without a driver's license
because of the last DUI, I prayed with a passion for
ESH to benefit others. I want to remind you GGG.
ESH seemed like a common sense thing to pray for. I
prayed for the right words to come out of my mouth
at a meeting that would help at least one person
follow through with their recovery. I prayed in the
affirmative and thanked God for working on things
behind the scenes. That six months, I had a few slips

along the way, but they were all while walking on the ice to a meeting. One night, almost all of the walk was glare ice. TIT with an *M* was where I was at on those walks.

{T}otally

{I}n

{T}he

{M}oment. Just added a *T* to the front of ITM. Conscious contact with GOMU was a deliberate choice that turned into a habit. TIT with an M. TITM is where real sanity lies. Totally in the moment. It takes work in the societal jungle in which we live to stay in the moment. Remember our hit song which included the lyrics "People are crazy"? A person really has to focus on their own sanity when living in an insane world. Being a twelve steppin' creature helps matters tremendously.

Remembering the eleventh step acronym MIA, along with PS rather than using BS is a dynamite way of going about our daily lives, a whole lot less hulla-balloo. MIA leads to a PS sort of existence instead of the BS toxic death life which accompanies us when drinking.

MIA, PAD, and PUSH help us stay connected with our higher power. Focusing on keeping this channel of communication open enables saner, more intuitive responses in all we encounter.

Intuition, that voice within. God-consciousness leads us along magically. Like it says in *The Promises*, "We will intuitively know how to handle situations which used to baffle us." This becomes reality when the eleventh step is incorporated into our lives. My life experiences with this make me a true believer that this is the easier, softer ride down the road to recovery. There is less ping-pong playing in our heads when making decisions. Self-centered procrastination is less prevalent. Focusing on a God-centered directed life rather than our own self-centered ways leads us to more and more sanity.

Conscious contact with a God of our own understanding is our vehicle to sane decisions and therefore a saner lifestyle. Step 11 is always the key, that added effort for sanity. Having experienced such assistance, I can honestly say I would rather have God do my thinking than shoulder my burdens alone. Totally trusting in this spiritual connection leads to serenity, POM, and sanity. This trust alleviates our egotistical, insane, mind-developed fears. A harmony between yourself and your God is the magic of this spiritual connection.

Our very own prayer and meditation mix are what I consider to be in harmony with a God of our very own understanding. Prayer is simply; what we do when we talk with our higher power and meditation is stilling our minds and opening our spirits to God's influence.

Leaning on our intuition leads to more PS just like listening to our conscience does. Incidentally, I have read and heard it said by prominent writers and speakers that intuition and conscience are God's voice. That works with GOMU.

Conscience is ingrained in step 10. We grow a conscience when we live in step 10. That is, continuing to take personal inventory and when we were wrong promptly admitting it. In my mind, during my early months of soberness, I personalized step 10 by promptly admitting my wrongs along the way. Living step 10 by getting right with GOMU shortly after a misdeed. I looked up to the skies above and asked forgiveness from GOMU. One of those microwave prayer deals. Doing so was fantastic for my conscience building. It leads to more PS with a lot clearer mind. Amends were made to my victims the next time I saw them. I incorporated step 10 into my life before the middle six steps were barely glanced at. More on this move to come.

Step 12 does wonders for more sanity and PS in our lives. Having had a spiritual awakening as the result of these steps, we tried to carry this message to alcoholics and practice these principles in all our affairs.

Spiritual awakening discombobulated me for a while until I brought forth KISS,S to the limelight. This time meditating on two big words, the dictionary was not needed. KISS,S had taught me that our thinking is a big part of our spirituality. When we get up in the morning, don't we become awake? Awaken to another day? I now have even amplified my meaning of spiritual awakening to any change in spirit. I had thought God had to fall from the sky and land in my lap to experience a spiritual awakening. How about waking up to our morning meditation books as being a spiritual awakening? We are waking up to another day of life. Whatever we read affects our spirits for the day.

Morning meditation material is extraordinary ESH to share at meetings, taking some positive from our morning spiritual awakening and sharing with the group is living step 12. A good portion of it for sure. Carrying this message to alcoholics sounds a whole lot like the Preamble to me. Sharing the positive is magical, positive self-talk. When we speak to the group, we are also talking to ourselves out loud. I relate sharing ESH to a mindset of I did it. I did it. I did it. Similar to all the we wills in *The Promises* reading. Give it away to keep it at its finest. Special note: Taking a personal self-pity bath in front of the group will result in more self-pity and a poor attitude. Our speaking affects our thinking, and at the same time, our thinking affects our speaking.

Living steps 10 to 12 is essential when striving for a saner life. Around the AA table, I once heard it said that steps 10 to 12 are God's loving discipline. I must have needed a lot of discipline as I realized somewhere during the first six months to a year of sobriety that steps 10 to 12 had been incorporated into my daily living. All of this had taken place subconsciously. This is where I'll get back to the barely glanced at middle six steps.

No Nuts for Me

Let's now examine my reason for initially neglecting the middle six steps. What we are looking at here is the order in which I went through the steps. I don't believe this is meditated on near enough.

Steps 1 to 3 were done thoroughly during my forty-day stay for inpatient care. I really whistled the heads of two twenty-year career counselors with my step 2 dissertation to a class of sixteen. I got a start on step 4 during those forty days.

After inpatient and two weeks of outpatient, I became an AA animal. Ninety in ninety kind of thing. Journalizing those meetings, I was living steps 1 to 3 in my mind daily and had steps 4 and 5 on the back burner. Along the way, I heard a thirty-year sober queen tell the group that steps 4 to 5 were like getting naked with another person. Then I heard a twenty-five-year-old male vet of soberness suggest sharing bits and pieces of steps 4 to 5 here and there.

I decided on the bits and pieces approach rather than getting completely naked with my sponsor, a clergy, or a complete stranger. No writing is involved whatsoever. Ya baby. Back in my school days, it took me a half-hour to write a paragraph that made any sense. If I can write this book, all who WANT TO can recover. That old male vet suggested sharing step 4 as we go. Only share with people we are comfortable with. Sometimes it may be at a particular meeting. Sometimes a story with your sponsor. Maybe another story with an ordinary fellow AA-er. A newcomer may benefit immensely from a chunk of your step 4, especially when done one on one. Lyle, an AA buddy of mine, and I swapped many war stories back and forth while out in a boat fishing together during my first summer of sobriety. Now that's a whole lot more comfortable of a way of sharing portions of my war chest with anyone. No slaving over a hot pen to git 'er done.

NUTS

The order and how we go about the steps should not be scrutinized. I prefer to live them rather than just work them. No nuts for me.

{N}ot

{U}sing

{T}he

{S}teps. Working through the steps one at a time in order and then forgetting about them is a slower path to sanity. The more we live the steps, keeping them in our prevailing mindset, the saner we get. The twelve steps are our twelve cylinders that make up our fabulous sanity motor. For me, a sanity-driven life is the easier, softer ride. No NUTS for me.

As I have mentioned steps 1 to 3 have remained with me since my inpatient days. Remember HOW? Step 1 is that we must live with rigorous HONESTY to the fact our lives of the drink are insanity. Step 2 we must live with an OPENNESS to a power greater than ourselves to help us on our journey of recovery. Step 3 is the follow-through step. The action step.

To live/use step 3 in our daily lives requires a WILLINGNESS to surrender our will to that of God's will time and time again. All moments we encounter must have God's will and not ours as a backdrop. Doing so will lead to more PS. When I realized GOMU's will was not a decision made only once like the steps reads, I made a decision to turn our will and our lives over to the care of God as we understood him, instead being an ever-changing deal depending on life's bumps and jumps. We must continue with a spirit of trust and surrender in all. Making a choice to remain in God's will in all we do. This decision must be made over and over again throughout all our days. Because of a whole lotta contemplative thought, I learned God's immediate will for me could be different than that of his long-term will for me. Continuing in God's will is a choice from one moment to the next. No NUTS for me on this step. I wanted to focus on using/living step 3 for a sanity-driven life.

Steps 4 to 5 were being lived as pointed out earlier and at about the same time, it dawned on me to draw a line between my using life and my sober life. I decided to work on the wreckage of my partying life and my sober life in concert with one another. Steps 4 to 9 got adequate attention, and steps 10 to 12 became daily tools of mine. No NUTS for me. Pondering on steps 10 to 12 for a while during my infant SOS 1 days it occurred to me to incorporate them immediately into my life.

I strongly encourage all to start using steps 10 to 12 daily, today, if already not doing so. Step 10 starts with the word *continue*. That sounds like a lifetime deal to me. *Continue* means to keep doing something. I kept using step 10 daily, keeping both my sober life and using life happenings as inputs of personal inventory. I admitted wrongs and then dealt with them no matter which life the wrong attached itself to.

Step 11 is a must for recovery/saner life. If I am looking to PMS 2 and recover from alcoholism, I want all the help I can get. Step 11 was a no-brainer. No not using this step daily for me. I really started to meditate on the order we do steps because of step 11.

Prayer and meditation (PAM). It occurred to me that PAM could be useful to me for both patching up my past cocktail life and also help proceeding in my sober life. Don't tell me I must complete steps 1 to 10 before I can PAD and PUSH. To go through life MIA style. I was itching for that restoration of my sanity, so step 11 became part of my daily gig. At this time is when I put my pen down with the working idea of the steps and instead started using the steps regularly. My pen kept warm with my journalizing. I saw journalizing as MIA. I thought when I wrote.

Step 12 is excellent positive self-talk when we carry our message of ESH. Order of steps. I didn't wait to start carrying my message to the group. I brought my morning mediation and journalizing mindset to a meeting and shared it. I did it. I did it. I did it. I lived step 12, the carrying the message portion of it, right from the get-go. I went against meeting chatter suggesting we sit in the corner with our arms crossed and head down for the first year or so. To put cotton in our mouths and listen. I spat their cotton on the floor. There's no "I did it" with this suggestion. Remember when we talk to the group, we are also talking to ourselves.

I strongly encourage any length of sobriety people to share ESH. A one-day sober infant can tell people how they did it. Maybe it took three meetings that day to stay sober. Maybe they spent the entire day with a sponsor. Maybe they spent half a day with PAM, went to a meeting, and fellowshipped with their sponsor to boot. Whatever it took to conquer a day of nonuse is ESH that can be shared with the group as long as they stay out of the self-pity bath water. I did it. I did it. I did it.

11–3 is the Golden Key
11–3 is the Shift for Me

Using the six steps (1 to 3 and 10 to 12) regularly starting the first year of my sobriety is what I contribute my success to. Step 11 was half the golden key. My conscious contact with GOMU improved immensely the more I lived it. This required a conscientious decision and effort to do so. To stay focused I PAM for ESH along with microwave prayers of gratitude, insight, guidance, and direction, always praying in the affirmative.

Conscious contact became cosmic in nature when I prayed and meditated my way through the day. That's when the acronym TRIPLE *C* was birthed.

{C}osmic

{C}onscious

{C}ontact. The best way to describe it may be that of living in each moment of the day from one to the next. Totally in the here and now all day long.

TRIPLE *C* was the vehicle for riding the pink cloud during those days, and thereafter. Many a scholar have put a time limit relating to the pink cloud concept, that it can only last so long. My experience living life TRIPLE *C* style taught me otherwise. Looking back, it seems like for most of my first two years of soberness, I rode that cloud.

Happy, joyous, and free. Phase 4 mentioned in the *Big Book* kind of deal was how I felt and realized that the pink cloud ride could last indefinitely, as long as I kept my 3D glasses on instead of my beer goggles. Under them required loving eyes rather than lying eyes.

TRIPLE-*C*-style living took both loving eyes and 3D glasses over them. The three *D*'s are

{D}edication

{D}etermination

{D}iscipline. The more I lived this way, the saner I became and remained. During this time, life was much easier as intuition and conscience fueled a whole bunch of my life.

Living the abovementioned TRIPLE *C* style, I became more and more aware of my thinking.

I became more conscious of my every thought. Conscious contact with GOMU became much easier. I was now doing much more responding to life rather than reacting. MIA was now the rule, instead of the exception, for how I navigated my daily life. My days were made up of PS.

PM living became a byproduct of my TRIPLE *C* with GOMU. To keep in the PM I concocted another mind game which I played with myself. I should only look to the days with PM in mind and forget about the AM. If the here and now, PM is my goal then I should stay away from thinking about AM.

PM is not AM. My mind game was that AM represented

{A}nother

{M}oment or

{A}nxious

{M}oment. Neither of these AMs did I want a part of. My goal was to remain in the present moment. PM.

The PM is the here and now. More sanity goes along with living in the PM rather than living another moment which more often than not is also an anxious moment. There is no babble of noise in our heads of our past or future when kicking around in the PM. No mind chatter interference when we are consciously awake to the PM.

We can always talk ourselves back to the here and now. A fantastic self-talk affirmation to utilize when we find ourselves in that dangerous neighborhood of our own mind is, "The present moment is

NOW the focal point of my life." Saying this over and over again to ourselves WILL get us back to the present. What time is it? The time is NOW. The time is always the present moment, not another moment.

PM is another handy-dandy acronym to trigger recovery thoughts. The game of life is always played out in the here and now, not in our heads dwelling on the past or projecting into the future too far. Anyway we dice it up the time is always now, or in other words, the PM.

Another premo-self-talk ditty to keep us in the PM is, "I succeed by being in the moment…PERIOD."

I have heard and read from many sources the quickest way to get back to the moment is our breathing. Long, deep, natural breaths empty all from our minds. Seems to me I remember back in my earliest school days, someone telling me to take a deep breath when they knew I was upset about something. Our breathing can only be done at the moment, and when we concentrate on it, we are TITM. There is no past or future involved with breath concentration to discombobulate our PS of the moment.

When we are in the moment, we are

{T}otally

{P}resent (TP). Totally present is the sanest place to live.

The other half of the golden key for sanity to go along with step 11 is step 3. 11–3 IS THE GOLDEN KEY. 11–3 IS THE SHIFT FOR ME. 11–3 WILL SET ME FREE.

Step 3 bothered the hell out of me early on in sobriety. It reads as follows… "Made a decision to turn our will and our lives over to the care of God as we understand him." I was behooved to what God's will for me was. I struggled with the enormity of his will. I felt it needed to be some grandiose lifetime target to shoot for a way off in the future somewhere.

To keep with the spirit of KISS something as simple as staying sober became a thought of mine for being God's will for me. Can't we have a moment to moment God's will along with the grandiose and all moments along the way in between? Don't plans require the immediate and mid-stream moments to achieve the ultimate?

Life is a moment-to-moment deal that depends on circumstances that come and go throughout our days. Things often change drastically from one day to the next and even from one moment to another. These situational deviations require contemplative thought for us to remain in God's will. Responding to life rather than reacting to it will keep us closest to his will. His will is sanity. In God's will, PMS 2 is a given. Therefore, surrendering to God's will is better accomplished by living an MIA way of existence. Step 11, MIA, leads us to step 3, God's will. No NUTS for me. Eleven-to-three is the golden key. Step 11 keeps us closest to God's will.

To me surrendering to something was the weakling way of living before my recovery career. But as I motored down the road of recovery doing just that I found great comfort. I found that we can't change most circumstances we encounter in life. All we can really change is how we respond to them. Just AI. Nonacceptance is insane, therefore STTM. STTM is surrendering to the present.

My research leads me to the fact that God is the present. God is the moment. Living the eleven to three shift for me means contemplative thought/MIA in what I encounter throughout the day. God's will must be our differing situations during the day as GOD does not make any mistakes. If I respond to a given situation by doing the next right thing then I am living God's will. Step 3.

Surrendering to God's will is best accomplished by living in an MIA fashion. Living one day at a time. One moment at a time. Surrendering to HIS will each and every moment of our lives. Remembering the importance of self-talk I like to use the little gem, "MIA I go about my day." This song and dance keeps me in a responsive rather than reactive mode which leads to saner decisions and a whole lot less drama besides adhering to God's will. God's way is sanity. Using MIA for what the moment calls for is living the eleven-to-three shift.

PAM for ESH is a great way to stay closer to sanity/God's will. It keeps us in the mindset of being others-centered and not in the bad neighborhood of our own minds. Remembering that PAM is step 11 and others-centered, sharing ESH will always constitute God's will, step 3. One can see PAM for ESH does keep us in a good, sober vibe. I realized I was living the eleven-to-three shift early in sobriety.

Eleven-to-three does set us free. It frees us of our ego. It frees us from chaos. It frees us from tough decisions when conscience and intuition are trusted. It frees us from the drink. It frees us from insanity. Eleven-to-three is a lethal weapon for sanity. Intuition and conscience, divine intervention, in my opinion, guides us in making choices throughout the day. Saner decisions through and through. Eleven-to-three is the path to sanity because of the divine guidance we receive in our very own intuition and conscience. Intuition and conscience are greatly improved when living the eleven-to-three shift.

Eleven-to-Three Is the Path to Sanity and Sobriety

Sane decisions teaming up with appropriate actions will always keep us sober. With remaining *sober* being our number one priority, the word *sober* is the granddaddy acronym of them all.

{S}anity

{O}rientated

{B}ehavior

{E}quals

{R}ecovery. Our lives consist of one behavior after another, and Sanity-Orientated Behavior Equals Recovery for us alcoholics does lead to more sober moments and days. Thinking we can take a drink is insane and therefore doesn't jive with being a sane choice for us alcoholics. We can't even have one drink. To remain sober we must behave sanely toward that first drink. We can't think for a minute that we can have just one or a few. Sanity-orientated behavior, for us drunks, is refusing to take that first drink. I sip. I slip. I use. I lose. Now and always, I choose not to lose.

We, here and again, are reminded of the fact there is no graduation day for our recovery. Recovery is a lifetime agenda with no flash in the pan cure. Our only cure is to live with a sober spirit, keeping out that toxic spirit that leads us to spiritual bankruptcy. That old spirit, mindset, led us to insanity whereas our new sober spirit rewards us with continued recovery and sanity to boot. Our behavior is always a choice. We choose to behave this way or that. Keeping our sober acronym in mind we can see that sanity is one choice after another. Our days and moments differ from one to the next requiring us to make a decision, a choice, in regard to our changing circumstances. We must STTM. Respond, MIA, rather than react to it and then behave accordingly.

STTM requires total acceptance with no resistance to each moment that crosses our path on a given day. Surrendering to the present moment means we are totally conscious and awake to the here and now with no unneeded mind chatter of the past or future. There is no sanity in participating in mindless mind chatter. All happens in the present, not in our minds.

STTM is the easiest and sanest way of living. All we need to do is accept the moment. Ponder on it, MIA, and then respond according to our interest for sanity. When we **surrender to the moment**, we are surrendering to God at that moment. A God-tailored moment must be his will as nothing in his world happens by mistake. MIA/step 11, contemplative thought, brings us to step 3 (God's will). eleven-to-three is the path to sanity and more sobriety. Taking the first three letters of sobriety, we have SOB.

Long Haul It with SOB

SOB.
{S}anity
{O}riented
{B}ehavior. SOB is always ignoring that first drink. SOB is going to an AA meeting. SOB is hanging out with a good sponsor. SOB is morning meditation when meditating on the right material leads us to more sobriety and sanity. SOB is prayer and meditation. My SOB will always include golfing and fishing. All of the above are great sources of sanity.

SOB breaks trail for PMS 2. One SOB after another Protects My Sanity. Sanity and sobriety are a certainty when we live according to one SOB followed by the next. Prevailing personal sanity is the rule rather than the exception. Maintenance of this sober vibe will keep us sober.

Recovery is a *one-day-at-a-time* deal. Days are made of many moments; therefore days must be broken down to one moment at a time. Recovery and PMS 2 is a choice which is accomplished when SOB directs our behavior. One SOB after another. Choosing sane behavior one moment at a time will reward us with abundant sobriety and sanity. Recovery is choosing the correct SOB for any given moment.

About the Author

Doug Norgren grew up in Cloquet, Minnesota. After graduating from Cloquet High School, he went on to get a business management degree from the University of Minnesota, Duluth. From business management to book author. There's only one way that's possible—GOD.

One night living in the ghettos of Duluth, Doug had a 2:00 a.m. spiritual awakening. Out of a dead sleep, he was awakened by a voice, clear as can be. A stern, forceful voice spoke, saying, "Doug, write a book." That was his request from GOD, to write *KISS SPIRIT*. It was a new thing for Doug to do.

> See I am doing a new thing!
> Now it springs up. Do you not
> perceive it? I am making a way in
> the wilderness and streams in the
> wasteland. (Isaiah 43:19)

There's been a whole lot of wilderness and streams in Doug's life journey with more to come.

Both nature and nurture have played immense roles, and they still do.

Meditation, prayer, and reading are part of his life. Fantastic mind-food for thought nourishment. He still gets a thrill from catching a fish or stroking a good golf shot. Doug currently lives in Minnesota, waiting for the fishing opener and golf course to open.

www.ingramcontent.com/pod-product-compliance
Lightning Source LLC
Chambersburg PA
CBHW031355160726
47993CB00002B/978